Let's Look at Diggers and Dumpers

John Allan

HUNGRY TOMATO™

MINNEAPOLIS

Thanks to the creative team:
Editor: Tim Harris
Design: Perfect Bound Ltd

Hungry Tomato®
A division of Lerner Publishing Group, Inc.
241 First Avenue North
Minneapolis, MN 55401 USA

For reading levels and more
information, look up this title at
www.lernerbooks.com.

Main body text set in
Fibra One Alt.

Library of Congress Cataloging-in-Publication Data

Names: Allan, John, 1961– author.
Title: Let's look at diggers and dumpers / John Allan.
Other titles: Diggers and dumpers
Description: Minneapolis, MN : Hungry Tomato, a
division of Lerner Publishing Group, Inc., [2019] |
Series: Mini mechanic | Audience: Age 6–9. | Audience:
Grades K to 3.
Identifiers: LCCN 2018049643 (print) | LCCN
2018051360 (ebook) | ISBN 9781541555341 (eb pdf) | ISBN
9781541555334 (lb : alk. paper)
Subjects: LCSH: Excavating machinery–Juvenile
literature. | Dump trucks–Juvenile literature. |
Earthwork–Juvenile literature.
Classification: LCC TA735 (ebook) | LCC TA735 .A448 2019
(print) | DDC 621.8/65–dc23

LC record available at https://lccn.loc.gov/2018049643

Manufactured in the United States of America
1-45934-42828-1/18/2019

Contents

The Mini Mechanics

We sometimes use a mallet to break parts off a vehicle.

Screwdrivers are used to tighten screws.

We are the mini mechanics. Welcome to our workshop. We work on some amazing vehicles. Here are a few of the tools we use to fix them.

This is a hacksaw used for cutting through thin pieces of metal.

A good mechanic always needs a tape measure.

Excavators

There are lots of different types of excavators, and they come in all sizes. They are mainly used for digging. This one is called a backhoe.

For small holes and ditches, you need a mini excavator.

This long arm is called the boom.

This is called the dipper arm because it dips in and out of the ground.

These metal teeth make it easier to cut through the earth.

Dump Truck

Dump trucks can carry large loads and lift up so that the loads slide out. Some small dump trucks are called tipper trucks.

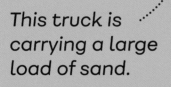

This truck is carrying a large load of sand.

The top board
protects the cab
from falling rocks.

This dump truck
has ten wheels and a
spare tire on the side.

Concrete Mixer

This truck makes and delivers concrete to building sites. Sand, gravel, water, and cement are mixed together to make the concrete.

This is the water tank.

Concrete pours out of the metal tube at the rear of the truck.

The drum turns about eight times a minute.

The cement, gravel, and sand are poured in here.

Crawler Excavator

Large excavators that have tracks instead of wheels are called "crawlers." The tracks help the excavator grip on muddy ground.

You have to climb up a ladder to get into the cab.

These large excavators are used for big jobs such as demolition, mining, and building roads.

This large bucket can move more than 500 shovelfuls of earth at a time.

13

Jackhammer

This excavator has a large drill on the end of its arm. It is used mainly for breaking up concrete.

This drill breaks concrete into smaller lumps that can then be removed easily.

Smaller pieces of concrete are broken up with a smaller jackhammer.

The excavator has stabilizers to keep it still as the drill goes up and down.

Road Roller

The road roller flattens new roads with its heavy metal rollers.

The roller has flattened some of the road, but the rest of the road is still rough.

A roller weighs the same as eighteen cars.

The roller can be filled with sand or water to make it heavier.

Bulldozer

Bulldozers push tree stumps, earth, and stones out of the way with a huge metal blade. They are clearing the ground for building. This is called dozing.

This dozer has tracks to help it move over muddy ground.

The blade is curved to help move the earth away.

This metal arm is called a
tilt ram. It lifts the blade up.

Road Paver

A paver spreads asphalt on the road. Asphalt is a mixture of hot tar and small stones. It is the top surface layer of most roads.

As the warm asphalt comes out, a metal plate spreads it into a thin layer.

First, a grader smoothes a flat layer of stones over the ground. Then the paver lays the asphalt.

The front of the paver is called a hopper and is where the asphalt is stored.

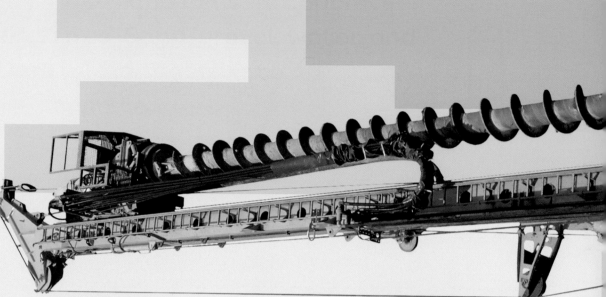

Hydraulic Drilling Machine

Hydraulic drilling machines are used to drill giant holes at construction sites. The drill is called an auger.

This construction site has three drilling machines digging holes for the foundation of a new building.

This ring holds the auger still as it drills into the ground.

This arm tilts the auger so it can drill straight into the ground or at an angle.

Glossary

blade: sharp cutting edge

cab: the place where the driver sits to drive a vehicle

concrete: building material made by mixing cement powder and water

demolition: the process of knocking down old buildings

foundation: the base of a building

grader: a machine for flattening earth

hydraulic: run using oil or water under pressure

workshop: a place where things are made or repaired